Page Turners

A New Song for Nina

Fiona Joseph

Series Editors:
Rob Waring and Sue Leather
Series Story Consultant: Julian Thomlinson
Story Editor: Sue Leather

Australia • Brazil • Canada • Mexico • Singapore • United Kingdom • United States

Page Turners Reading Library

A New Song for Nina

Fiona Joseph

Publisher: Andrew Robinson

Executive Editor: Sean Bermingham

Editorial Assistant: Dylan Mitchell

Director of Global Marketing: Ian Martin

Senior Content Project Manager: Tan Jin Hock

Manufacturing Planner: Mary Beth Hennebury

Contributor: Vessela Gasper

Layout Design and Illustrations: Redbean Design Pte Ltd

Cover Illustration: Eric Foenander

Photo Credits:
54–55 (top) Anastasios71/Shutterstock
54 (bottom) Veronika Rumko/Shutterstock
56–57 (top) antb/Shutterstock
57 (bottom) Ashley Pickering/Shutterstock
58 auremar/Shutterstock
59 Narcis Parfenti/Shutterstock

ISBN-13: 978-1-4240-4659-1

ISBN-10: 1-4240-4659-9

National Geographic Learning
20 Channel Center Street
Boston, Massachusetts 02210
USA

Cengage Learning is a leading provider of customized learning solutions with office locations around the globe, including Singapore, the United Kingdom, Australia, Mexico, Brazil, and Japan. Locate your local office at: **www.cengage.com/global**

Visit National Geographic Learning online at **NGL.Cengage.com**

Visit our corporate website at **www.cengage.com**

Printed in Mexico
Print Number: 02 Print Year: 2021

Contents

Review

Background Reading

People in the story

Nina Cross
a twenty-five-year-old woman who loves music

Craig Talbot
a twenty-five-year-old drummer in a band and Nina's ex-boyfriend

Jon Pritchard
a twenty-seven-year-old businessman

Marsha Black
a twenty-five-year-old woman and Nina's best friend

The story takes place in a town near Manchester, England.

LIVE
BREAK DOWN
CLUB

Chapter 1

Going to see a band

It was seven o'clock in the evening. Nina was waiting for her friend Marsha outside a club in a town near Manchester. She looked at her watch. Marsha was twenty minutes late. Nina took her phone out to see if her friend had sent a message. No, there was nothing.

Nina heard the beat of the music from inside the club. The band was already playing, and she didn't want to miss another minute. She had heard good things about this group, Breakdown. It wasn't her fault that Marsha was late. Nina went inside.

"One ticket for Breakdown," she said. "I'm not too late, am I? Please."

"No, but the doors are closing now," the man replied.

Nina went to the rooms downstairs. The sound of music was loud in her ears, and the stage lights flashed brightly in her eyes. She loved this moment, when the sound filled her head and her heart, and she forgot everything apart from the music.

She looked at the people in the audience to see their reaction. They were jumping in time to the beat and waving their arms in the air. *This band is really good,* Nina thought. She found a table and chairs and sat down at the back of the room.

The song finished. The lead singer said to the crowd, "Are you having fun?"

The crowd cheered.

"ARE-YOU-HAVING-FUN?" he said again.

The audience cheered even louder.

Yes, thought Nina, *this band, Breakdown, is perfect.* She took out her book and began writing in it.

Five minutes later, Marsha arrived. "I'm so sorry, Nina," she said. "My train was late."

But Nina hardly noticed. She was too busy listening to the music and making notes. Marsha went to buy some drinks. When she returned, the band was taking a break for a few minutes.

Marsha raised her glass, smiled, and said to Nina, "Well done for getting your new job. How's it going so far?"

Nina smiled. "I love it!" she said, excitedly. "It's like my dream has come true." Nina felt lucky. She was well known as a music blogger, writing reviews of all the bands she went to see. And then she was offered a job working for the Jambox Music Festival in her hometown. She had to find new groups with great potential—those who could be future stars—to play at the festival.

"It doesn't feel like work," she said. "I can come and listen to all the bands I like."

Marsha laughed to see her friend's excitement. "Have you found any good ones yet?"

"Yes, I've got nine bands already. I just need one more." Nina looked at her ticket for Breakdown. "You know, these guys would be great for the festival. I'll speak to them after the show and ask them if they'll play for us."

The band played their last song. It was a slow love song

with just the singer and the two guitarists. The young man on the drums put down his sticks and drank from a bottle of water. Then he took off his hat and his dark glasses, and cleaned his face and neck with a towel.

Nina looked at the drummer. "I don't believe it," she said in surprise.

"What is it?" Marsha asked.

"That guy . . . the drummer . . . I know him. I mean, I used to know him."

"Really? How?"

"That's Craig. He was my first boyfriend."

BREAK
DOWN

Chapter 2

A broken heart

Nina sat back in her seat.

"You look really strange," Marsha said. "Do you want to go outside?"

"No, I'm OK. Just let me sit here for a minute."

Nina couldn't believe it. She hadn't seen Craig for three years, since she was twenty-two. She hadn't had a serious boyfriend after Craig.

"So what happened between you two?" Marsha asked.

Nina spoke quietly. "Nothing much . . . he just broke my heart, that's all," she said with a small smile.

Marsha said, laughing, "Broke your heart? Really? You never told me about him before." But she saw Nina's face and then Marsha spoke with kindness. "Do you want to tell me about it?"

Breakdown had gone off the stage. But now they came back to do an encore. The crowd cheered loudly. Nina waited for the noise to stop before she spoke again.

"I fell in love with Craig when I was seventeen. We met in college. He was the same age as I, and we had a lot in common."

"Let me guess," Marsha said. "Music?"

Nina nodded. "We liked the same bands, the same kind of music. He was a really good drummer, too. Then he was asked to join a band. He was so happy and excited."

"How about you?"

"I was really pleased for him. Everyone told him how wonderful he was . . ."

"But . . . ?"

"Oh, I don't know. Things started to change between us. He couldn't see me as much. He always had a gig to play in different cities. I said, 'Take me with you, so I can see you play,' but he didn't want to."

"What an idiot," Marsha said. "Him, I mean, not you!"

Nina continued. "Then one day the band was offered a contract with a record company. The only problem was . . . it was in Australia. I wanted to go with him, but my parents said I had to stay here and go to the university."

"So Craig left you here in England?"

"Yes," Nina said. "He decided we should break up and both be free."

Marsha put her jacket on. "Well, that was good advice," she said. "You did fine without him. Look at you now. You have your dream job, doing what you love."

"But I thought Craig was in Australia! What's he doing in England?"

"Maybe the record contract didn't happen. Don't worry about that. The only thing you need to decide is if you want Breakdown to play at the festival."

The festival! Nina had forgotten all about it. She was too busy thinking about Craig. But Marsha was right. Breakdown was a great band, and she should book them for the festival. She stood up.

"Where are you going?" her friend asked.

"I'm going backstage," Nina said. "I'm going to talk to them about playing at the festival. Wait for me outside the club."

"OK," Marsha said. "If you're sure you can handle seeing Craig again . . ."

Nina drank from the glass of juice in her hand. "I'm fine, honestly. Stop worrying! I don't care about Craig any more. I'm OK without him, like you said."

She walked up to the door of the band's dressing room. She heard the young men talking and laughing inside. They had enjoyed themselves. Nina stood outside the door and knocked. No reply. She knocked again more loudly, and the door opened. There he was. Craig was standing in the doorway. He looked at her for a moment and then his face looked surprised. "Nina?"

She nodded, smiling. He held the door open and she went inside.

Chapter 3

Nina makes a decision

"So what happened next?" Marsha said, pulling on Nina's arm as they walked home from the club. Nina was almost dancing with excitement, and Marsha walked quickly as she tried to keep up with her.

"He couldn't believe it," Nina said. "He was really surprised to see me. I met the other band members—they were all really nice guys. I told Craig about the festival and wrote my number down for him. And he gave me their manager's phone number and email so I could arrange it properly. Wouldn't it be great if Breakdown could play?"

"Great for the festival, or for you?" Marsha said, smiling.

"I'm going home to update my blog." Nina couldn't stop smiling. "Look at this photo I took with my phone." She showed Marsha a picture of herself and Craig standing close to each other.

At home, Nina got an orange juice and two chocolate biscuits and sat down at her laptop. She opened a new blog page. She was going to write a review of the evening and Breakdown's music.

"Breakdown is an amazing new band," she typed. "We hope to book them for the Jambox Festival on August 1. We have an exciting lineup, including bands such as Xray and Starlight in the Storm."

Nina bit into her biscuit and carried on writing her review. She uploaded the photograph of Craig and her, and typed underneath: *Nina Cross meets drummer Craig backstage.*

After an hour she checked her mobile phone, but Craig had not sent her a message yet.

The next day was the meeting to plan the Jambox Festival. The main organizer was Richard Fox, and he would want to know which bands Nina had chosen for the lineup. She opened a computer document with the list of names of all the bands she had seen so far. Xray was at the top. They were the most popular band and they had played at the festival many times. Perhaps she could let Breakdown be their support band. She typed in Breakdown under Xray.

The phone rang. She hoped it was Craig. It wasn't. It was Xray's manager. "Hi, Nina. Sorry to ring you so late. I want to tell you that Xray can play at the festival this year for sure."

"That's great," Nina said. "We've got a great support band for you. They're called Breakdown and they're a new . . ."

"Sounds great, Nina. Sorry, got to go. Talk soon."

Nina decided to ring Breakdown's manager, Terry. She called the number hoping that Craig might answer.

"Yes?" a deep voice said.

"Umm . . . hi," she said. "Is that Terry? It's Nina Cross here. We met tonight . . . well, I mean, I met Craig tonight at . . . umm . . ." Oh no, she was so nervous! "Craig said that Breakdown will play at the Jambox Festival. The date is August 1."

"Did he say that? He didn't tell me! I've never heard of the Jambox Festival. How do I know it's a serious festival?"

"Oh, it's been running for a number of years."

"How big is it?"

"Last year there were about two thousand people . . ."

"Pretty small, then."

"But this year we're going to sell twice as many tickets."

"Even so . . . it still sounds . . ."

Nina felt desperate. "I can promise you top billing," she said, suddenly. The best bands always played last.

They talked a little more. Nina tried to persuade him. Finally, Terry said, "Well, OK, we might have a deal—if you promise us the best time slot."

"Of course."

Nina said good-bye and ended the call. Yes, she had done it. She had booked Breakdown for the festival. She returned to her file and changed the order of the bands. Breakdown was now at the top, and Xray was their support act. It was time a new band had the chance to get top billing for a change; Xray might not like it, but she knew Richard, the festival organizer, trusted her to choose the best lineup.

Now all she had to do was to check out the site where the festival took place every year. The usual venue for the Jambox Festival was in the fields around Huntley Manor, an old mansion that was the home of Sir Wilfred Huntley. Nina had never met Sir Wilfred, but people said he was a kind and sweet old man. She looked forward to meeting him.

But it was time for bed now. She closed her eyes and went to sleep thinking of Craig.

Chapter 4

Huntley Manor

Nina woke early. She had a text from Marsha: "Do you want to go for a coffee this morning?" Nina texted back: "Sorry, going to a meeting about Jambox this morning. Maybe later? N x"

Nina took a shower and got dressed in jeans and a gray sweatshirt. She didn't need to look stylish.

Half an hour later, Nina arrived at the meeting. "Hi, Richard," she said to the organizer. She said hello to the other people on the festival team. They all looked very serious. Nina was worried. She wondered what the problem was. Surely they didn't know already that she had given Xray's time slot to Breakdown? She would say, "We need a brand new act instead of the same old bands."

She opened her mouth to speak, but then Richard said, "Nina, there's some bad news, I'm afraid. Sir Wilfred has died."

"Oh, that's sad," Nina said. "I heard he was a really nice man."

"Yes, he was," Richard continued. "A new owner has already bought Huntley Manor. We may not be able to have the field for the Jambox Festival this year. We may have to cancel the whole thing."

"But we can't do that," Nina cried. "There must be another way!"

The others all shook their heads.

She excused herself to go to the washroom. She looked in the mirror, glad to be alone with her thoughts. She was disappointed that the festival might not go ahead—no, more than disappointed.

She went back to the meeting and sat down. Richard raised his eyebrows, checking if Nina was all right. She nodded.

Richard spoke, "We know a little bit about the new owner of Huntley Manor. His name is Jon Pritchard. He's quite a young man." Richard looked around the room. "Perhaps we could ask him . . ."

". . . if we can still use the field?" Nina said quickly. "Of course we should."

"Well," Richard said, "he might want to use the land for his own projects, which may not include a festival."

"Yes," said one of the others. "I heard he wanted to build houses on it, or . . ."

"There's only one way to find out," Nina said. "Give me Mr. Pritchard's details. I'll go and see him right now."

Chapter 5

Meeting Mr. Pritchard

It was a long way to Huntley Manor. Nina was glad she was on her bike. Going by bike was faster than walking, and she wanted to get there as quickly as possible. The mansion was a huge and very old building with large fields at the back.

The front door was open, so she went inside. There was a large reception area for visitors, with a man sitting at a desk.

"Can I help you?" he said.

"Yes, I'm looking for a Mr. . . ." Nina looked at her notes. "Jon Pritchard. Is he here?"

"What time is your appointment?"

Nina said, "Appointment? I don't have one."

"In that case, I'm sorry . . ."

"I need to see him now," Nina said. "It's extremely important."

"And your name is . . . ?"

"Nina Cross." She looked around. Where was he?

Then a young man came into the reception. He looked about twenty-six or twenty-seven, and he was dressed in a stylish suit, with a shirt and tie. He looked slightly annoyed. "Is there a problem?" he said.

"Are you Mr. Pritchard? Look, can I see you?" Nina said.

"It's very important."

"Yes, of course. Come into my office."

They went into his office and he sat behind his large desk.

"So, how can I help you, Miss . . . ?"

"Cross. Nina Cross." Nina then explained about the Jambox Festival. "Sir Wilfred always let us use his fields for the festival, but now you're the new owner . . ."

"Ah, so you want to book the land? What date are you thinking of?"

"August 1." Nina waited, holding her breath.

Jon Pritchard looked at his diary. "OK, that's four months away. I don't see any problem with that. Let's go outside and you can tell me what you need for your festival."

Nina breathed. It looked like everything would be OK!

The two of them walked through the house. It really was very beautiful with its old wooden floors and paintings on the walls. They arrived at the back terrace, where the fields went farther and farther for almost a kilometer. There was plenty of space—it would be perfect. She couldn't wait to tell the committee that she had gotten the land successfully.

Breakdown could play their gig in the nearest field, close to the back of the house. Nina imagined the gig being over, everyone happy after a successful show, Craig asking her to come onto the stage where he would thank her, and then . . .

"Miss Cross?"

"Sorry, yes," she said. It was time to focus. "What do we need? I'd like to put one stage here," she said, pointing to an area close to the terrace, "and another over there. And we need a power supply, of course. Sir Wilfred usually let the musicians get ready in the house. He also gave the bands refreshments, you know, something to eat and drink, or so I was told. Would you be able to do that?"

Jon Pritchard nodded and took some notes on his phone.

When they got back to the office, he asked her to sit down again. He connected his phone to the computer.

"I've written down everything you've asked for," he said. "I'll email the documentation over to you tomorrow—unless you'd prefer to come here again?—and we can go from there."

"Thank you so much," Nina said excitedly. "I can come back tomorrow, no problem. In fact, I'd like to look around the field again and get started right away."

"Of course. I'll see you in the morning."

Well, that was easy, Nina said to herself, as she went toward the door.

On her way out, her phone rang. It was Richard.

"Hi," she said.

"You sound happy. How was the meeting?"

"Wonderful! Jon Pritchard says we can use the fields and the house."

"Great! Well done, Nina!"

Chapter 6

An unpleasant surprise

The next day, Nina returned to Huntley Manor and sat down in Mr. Pritchard's office. He gave her a folder. "Have a look at this and tell me what you think."

Nina looked inside the folder and saw pages and pages! The last page had a long list of figures and a total at the end. She looked at the headings.

HIRE OF LAND, she read. REFRESHMENTS. STAGE HIRE. And what was CONVENIENCES? She didn't understand.

"Now," Jon Pritchard said. "How do these numbers look to you? Are they OK for your budget?"

"My what?"

"Your budget," he said. "The amount of money you can spend."

"I know what a budget is," she said, hotly, "but I don't understand why you've given me this." Unless, she thought . . .

"Let me explain," he said, looking over her shoulder. "The stage and the electricity generator will be this amount." He pointed to a figure.

Seven hundred pounds? Was he joking?

"And what's this? Refreshments?" Nina asked. Three hundred pounds!

"You said you wanted food and drink for the musicians

while they get changed. And also for the other people working on the day?"

"Well yes, but . . ."

"And the conveniences if people need to use the bathroom. We can hire public toilets."

"But all that adds up to over two thousand pounds!"

"Like I said, what's your budget?"

"Well, I thought . . ." She stopped. "Sir Wilfred let us have the fields and land without paying. And he gave people refreshments for free. He even let people use the bathrooms inside the manor house."

Mr. Pritchard didn't speak for a few moments. Then he said, "I see. Do people pay to come and watch the bands at the festival?"

"Well, yes," Nina said. "But we need to make payments to the band members. And we need money to advertise the festival. If we give you this money, we'll have nothing left—it will be impossible. Can't you let us have the land for free and help us with the other costs?"

"I can't do that, I'm afraid," Jon Pritchard said.

Nina's face was red.

"Look," he said, "you can pay the money in parts. Pay 20 percent now and the rest after the festival when you've sold the tickets. That's very fair."

Nina stood up quickly. There was no point talking to Mr. Pritchard any longer.

"I'm sorry," she said, as calmly as possible, "but we'll have to find somewhere else to hold the festival. We don't have any other choice. Good-bye." As she left the office, the door banged shut behind her. *Too bad*, she thought.

Chapter 7

Thinking things over

Nina walked quickly out of Huntley Manor. She needed to be outside. *What a mean and horrible man,* she thought. The festival wouldn't make thousands of pounds. Jon Pritchard was crazy to think that.

Jambox was a music festival for young indie bands. Singers, guitarists, drummers—they cared more about making music than making money. That was the important thing. Jon Pritchard couldn't understand that—all he thought about was making money for himself.

Just then her phone rang. It was Richard again. She turned off her phone; she didn't want to speak to him until she had decided what to do. The only answer was to find another venue. Fast.

Back home, Nina sat at her computer. *Now think,* she told herself. *Where's a good place to have a festival?* There was another building like Huntley Manor about three kilometers away. She could try that. She could also ask her friends in the music business. Or they could even hold the festival in different places in the town. *Yes,* she thought, *that's a good idea. That would be different this year.*

Her computer beeped, telling her she had a new email. Was it from Craig? No, it was a message from Jon Pritchard. What did *he* want? She opened the email and read it.

f(x) Σ =
B
C
D
July £200
Aug £200
Sept £200
Oct £200
Nov £200
Dec £200
Jan £200
Feb £200
Mar £200
Apr £200
May £200
June £200
July

"Dear Miss Cross,

Thank you very much for coming to see me today to discuss the use of Huntley Manor for your music festival. I realize you had a shock when you saw the full costs. I am sorry for that. Please see the payment plan, which I have included. I hope this is helpful. Please call me to discuss your needs.

Best wishes,

Jon Pritchard"

She opened the document on her computer. It was a list of dates: July, August, September, going up to the following July. Next to each month was an amount of money. Feeling angry, she said to herself, *I don't need you or your stupid payment plan.*

She took a can of juice from the kitchen. Then she went back to her computer and began to search for venues and rooms to hire. She'd show Jon Pritchard that she didn't need to depend on him for help. She looked at his email again and pushed the delete key.

Chapter 8

More trouble for Nina

Nina woke up. The first thing on her mind was the festival and the problem of where to hold it. She hadn't found anywhere last night. She got out of bed, got an orange juice, and made a hot cheese sandwich. It was Saturday and she didn't have to go to the office. She took her breakfast back to bed and switched on her phone.

A text message from Craig—at last!

"Hi babe, how are the plans going for the festival? Can't believe we've got top billing! I've put the date on our website. It's at Huntley Manor, right? Let me know for sure. Love, Craig x"

For a moment Nina forgot about the problems with the festival and Mr. Pritchard. She read the message again. Craig had written "Love" and signed it with a kiss. That must mean something. *Did he still have feelings for me?* she wondered. Maybe he was sorry for the way their relationship had ended.

Enough, she told herself. There was no time to dream about Craig. She would save that for later. She must sort out the venue today and then she'd call him back.

She also had a missed call from Richard. She played the message.

"Hi Nina, hope things are OK. I'm starting on the advertising for the festival today . . . you know, the posters and the website announcement . . . Great news that we've got the venue from Mr. Pritchard. You did really well. He can be difficult, I heard, so good work. Any problems just call me. Bye."

Nina groaned. She had to get on the phone and speak to other venue owners. It was going to be a long weekend, she thought. Nina looked at her list of possible venues. She called the phone number of the first one—a large hall that was close by.

"Good morning, I'm Nina Cross. I want to book your hall for a music festival in August."

Nina listened while the lady gave her some figures.

Three thousand pounds? That's more than Huntley Manor!

"Oh, I see," Nina said. "No, I'm afraid that's more than our budget." She tried the next number on her list, but that venue was closed in August. That was no good. Nina crossed it off. The last phone number was for a venue a few kilometers out of town—not perfect but it was the best she could do. She called and spoke to the manager.

"The venue is free in August . . ."

Yes! thought Nina.

". . . apart from one day when the venue is not available. Let me check that for you. That's Saturday, August 1. We can't do that day, I'm afraid."

Nina ended the call. What was she going to do now? Why had she offered to talk to Jon Pritchard? Was it because she wanted to impress everyone? Well, they wouldn't be impressed when they found out they had no venue at all!

She called Marsha. "You've got to help me. I've got a real problem."

"What's the matter?" Marsha was worried.

Nina told her everything about the meeting with Jon Pritchard.

"You mean you didn't like his offer so you got mad and walked out? Your name is Cross for a good reason!"

"It's not funny," Nina said. "What shall I do?"

"Well, you need a venue or the festival won't happen."

"I know that!"

"Shall I tell you what I think? You won't like it, though."

"Go on," Nina said.

"Jon Pritchard made a good offer to you."

"But, Marsha, the festival never paid for the venue before! Sir Wilfred let Huntley Manor be used for free and he paid most of the other costs."

"Yes, but think about it from his point of view," Marsha said.

"Why should I? He's probably rich. He has enough money to let us use the land."

"How do you know that, Nina? In fact, he may not be rich at all. Just think—he spent a lot of money to buy Huntley Manor. Of course he wants to make some money back. He has to."

"I can't believe you're saying that. You should be on my side!" Nina wanted to throw the phone on the floor.

Even Marsha, her best friend, didn't understand her point of view.

Chapter 9

Call me Jon

An hour later, Nina put on her running shoes and picked up her music player. She went to the park to run—she needed to forget about her problems and running always helped. After twenty minutes she stopped and sat down on a wooden seat.

One of Breakdown's songs was playing. It was her favorite track on the CD Craig had given her. It was called "Are You the One?" She turned up the volume. As she listened, she started to imagine that Craig had written it just for her.

"Don't let your pride get in the way

I'd be so glad if you could stay."

The answer to her problem was clear. The only way for the festival to happen was for her to see Jon Pritchard again and say yes to his offer. And then she and Craig might have a chance to be together.

"You look nice," Marsha said, the next time they met. "Where are you going?"

"I'm going to see Jon Pritchard."

Nina was dressed in a smart suit. This time she meant business.

"Wish me luck," Nina said, as she put her arms around Marsha.

"Good luck, Nina, and I hope the meeting goes better than before," Marsha replied with a smile on her face.

Nina walked into the reception at Huntley Manor. She said, clearly, "I'm here to see Mr. Pritchard. Can you tell him it's Nina Cross?"

He suddenly appeared. "Nina, good morning! Call me Jon," he said in a cheerful voice. "Go into my office and have a seat. I'll get you a drink. Coffee? Tea? An orange juice, perhaps?"

Nina didn't know why he was so happy; probably he was delighted she needed his help after all! "A glass of water will be fine," she said. "Thank you," she added. She went inside his office.

On his desk was a large folder with "Nina Cross/ Festival" on it. She looked in the folder. There were papers with even more figures—he certainly loved his business plans.

"So, Nina, I'm pleased you changed your mind."

It was difficult, but she mustn't get cross this time. She said nothing.

"I looked at the figures again," he said. "Last time you said people pay to come to the festival—is that right?"

"Yes," Nina said. "Why?"

"Because if you add £1 to the cost of the ticket and you sell a thousand tickets . . . then that's an extra thousand pounds. If you add £2 to the cost . . ."

"Yes, I do understand that," Nina said. *I'm not a complete idiot,* she wanted to say. But actually it was a good idea.

Why hadn't she thought of doing that?

"And I've cut the cost by 55 percent," Jon continued. "I won't make any profit at all myself. But I don't mind. I want to help you."

"Thanks. That's good of you." Nina stood up. "Well, if that's all then . . . I'll say good-bye."

"Good luck with the rest of the planning, Nina. And, you never know, I might come along to the festival myself."

Later that evening, Nina met Marsha for a drink. She told her friend the good news about Huntley Manor and how impressed Richard was when he saw the plan.

"And," Nina said, "Jon Pritchard even said he might come to the festival. I can't imagine him enjoying it at all. He looks about twenty-seven, but he acts like a boring old businessman twice his age! I can't see him in a dirty, muddy field in his smart shoes and his suit!"

Marsha smiled.

"What?" Nina said.

Marsha answered, "For someone who hates Jon Pritchard, you talk about him a lot!"

"Don't be silly," Nina said. *Craig's the only man I'm interested in,* she thought. She was counting the weeks until the festival in August.

Chapter 10

A week to go

The next few weeks passed very quickly. Nina, Richard, and the others were all busy with the final plans for the Jambox Festival. There was still a lot to do before the big day.

Nina was late going to bed most nights, but before she went to sleep she always checked her phone for messages. Each time she had a text from Craig she was happy—even though he was only asking questions about the festival. More than once, she told herself, *Stop daydreaming about him and get on with your work.*

Soon there was only one week to go. *Only one week until I see Craig again,* she thought. When they broke up three years ago, she had tried not to think about him at all. It hurt too much. But now . . . now they had a chance to be friends again. She could admit she had never really gotten over him.

At the next meeting, Richard passed around the posters for the festival.

"They look amazing!" Nina said. Breakdown was the act right at the top. Craig would be very happy about that. She'd emailed him a copy of the poster but he had not replied yet. Never mind—she would see him soon.

"Well done to Nina," Richard said. "You got the venue for us. And it was a great idea to increase the ticket price. We should have enough money to pay Mr. Pritchard for the costs now."

Nina smiled. She didn't say that it had been Jon's plan. She would tell Richard, but not yet!

Her phone rang. "Excuse me," she said to the others. She went out into the hall.

"Is that Miss Cross?" The man on the phone sounded very angry indeed. She knew his voice. It was the manager of Xray.

"I've just seen the posters for the festival. Why are we the second act, below Breakdown?" he asked. "Who on earth are they? I've never even heard of them."

Nina felt bad. She knew that Xray wouldn't be happy being second. She had to think of a good reason to explain why.

"We . . . I mean, I . . . thought it would be better for you if you play before Breakdown. People will leave early, so it's a good time for you." Nina knew it wasn't true, but she went on talking and finally the manager didn't sound so angry. Phew.

Her phone rang again.

"Yes?"

"Hi, Nina, it's Craig. How's it going? Is everything ready for the festival? I can't wait for it—and to see you, too," he added.

"We could meet up when it's over . . . go for a drink?" Nina said, hopefully. Her heart was beating loudly.

"Cool, great idea," Craig replied.

"Where are you staying?"

"I think our manager has booked a hotel close by . . ."

"That's good," Nina said. *We could go for a late night drink after the show,* she thought.

Craig said, "I'm looking forward to seeing you again. You've changed a lot. You're really successful now. I'm impressed."

Nina smiled to herself—she liked hearing Craig say nice things about her.

"Will there be any agents there?" Craig asked.

"Agents?"

"You know, people who can get us a record deal."

Oh no, she'd forgotten all about contacting agents!

"I'll see what I can do," she said.

"You're wonderful. Sorry, babe, got to go now. See you in a week."

Nina went back into the meeting, trying hard to look serious. But she just wanted to smile.

Chapter 11

The big day arrives

Nina didn't think she would sleep the night before the festival. She was wrong. She woke up after a deep sleep and was ready for the day ahead. Richard had told her, "It's hard work at the festival. Make sure you take some food and drink with you. And don't forget to eat!"

She took a shower and dressed in her jeans and a nice top. She checked that her apartment was tidy. There was some pasta and tomato sauce in the kitchen—it was Craig's favorite food. Nina had cooked it the night before in case Craig was hungry after the gig. He might want a meal at her apartment.

Nina arrived at Huntley Manor. The atmosphere was busy. The electricians were setting up the equipment on the stage. The stallholders selling burgers and fries were already cooking. The delicious smell of food came in her direction.

An hour later, all of the bands had arrived except for Breakdown. Nina hoped that there had not been a car accident, or some other problem. She showed the bands into the house, where they could relax before their shows. In the field far away, she saw a man who looked like Jon Pritchard. Yes, it was him. So he kept his promise—he was here after all! As he came closer, Nina saw he was dressed in a sweatshirt and jeans with sneakers on his feet. He looked very different from when he was in a suit. His hair was a bit untidy, too, but she liked it.

USIC FESTIVAL

"Hi, Nina, how are you? It's coming together. You planned it all very well." Nina knew that wasn't quite true but she hoped he would say it again—in front of Craig next time!

At two o'clock in the afternoon, the first band began to play. There were two guitarists and a keyboard player and they were good. Not as good as Breakdown, Nina thought, but the whole point of the Jambox Festival was to give young bands a chance.

Jon came over again. "I brought you a drink," he said, giving her a cup of coffee.

"Just what I need! Thank you."

"And," he said, "I got you this. It's only a sandwich, I'm afraid, but it's better than nothing." Nina opened the paper bag. The bread was fresh and it was filled with tuna and cucumber.

"That's my favorite sandwich," she said, laughing. "How did you know?"

"Lucky guess," he said. "Come and sit down. You need a rest."

Nina sat on the grass and relaxed. It was wonderful to feel the grass on her feet. She smiled happily.

"You look very pleased with yourself," Jon said, smiling too.

"Oh, I am. Music means everything to me. It makes me happy. And I love helping new bands. These bands playing today are the stars of the future. At least some of them will be."

"It's really important to you, isn't it?"

"I've loved music ever since I was a child and my mother used to play the guitar to me."

"But what would you like to do in the future? Become a band manager?"

"I don't know. I'm happy doing what I want at the moment."

Nina looked around. She saw a small white truck coming down the road.

"Ooh look! Breakdown is coming, at last!" She got to her feet quickly.

"Thank you for the drink and sandwich, Jon. It was very kind of you. And I feel much better." She walked quickly to where the truck was parked, putting some lipstick on her lips and tidying her hair as she walked. Nina knew that Marsha would laugh if she saw her. But she couldn't help it. She wanted to look nice for Craig. And now the moment that she had spent many weeks thinking about was here.

The truck windows were open and she heard voices coming from inside.

"What a small venue! I can't believe we agreed to play here!"

Nina felt very cold suddenly. Surely that wasn't Craig talking like that. She must have misheard. She went to the front of the truck. Craig said, in surprise, "Nina! How are you? Sorry we're late. We had trouble on the roads."

"Shall I show you where you need to go?" she said. They walked side by side toward the house, their arms touching occasionally, while the other band members followed behind.

"I'm really excited you're playing today. I was listening to the CD you gave me. You have some great songs."

"Really? What's your favorite?"

"I like 'Are You the One?'" Nina said, suddenly feeling embarrassed.

Craig looked pleased. "I wrote that song. Terry, our manager, says if we could get a record deal, that song could go to number one. We just need that lucky break."

She wanted to tell him what the song meant to her, but now was not the right time.

Nina showed Craig and the others to one of rooms inside Huntley Manor. "You can use this place to relax and get changed before the gig later. I'll leave you to it."

She turned to go. "Oh, Nina," Craig said. "I've got something for you. I left it in the truck. Come with me to get it."

She took a deep breath and said, "Sure, let's go." At last, they were on their own. Craig took out something from the back seat and gave it to Nina.

"What's this?" she asked.

"Open it," he said.

"It's a CD," she said in surprise. "But you've already given me a copy."

"No, this is a DVD. It's got a film of us playing live. I was hoping you could give it to that agent you said was coming. Tell him what a great band we are, and why you chose us to play at the festival, etc."

"I see," Nina said, slowly.

Now was the time to tell him the truth. "I only said an agent *might* be here, Craig. I don't know for sure. We're quite a small festival so it wasn't a certainty."

"But you said there would be an agent," Craig said.

"Well, I didn't promise for sure." Nina had to ask the question, "Was that the only reason you came?"

Craig didn't reply. He looked down at the ground.

She spoke again. "So, there wasn't any other reason for coming to the festival?" Still no reply. Nina looked across the field. One of the Jambox posters had come off the wall and was blowing in the wind across the ground. She turned away from Craig, sick with disappointment.

I'm such an idiot, Nina said to herself. Tears came into her eyes. Craig hadn't changed. He was always more interested in his music than in her. But she had made the same mistake all over again.

She had to forget her feelings, she thought, wiping her tears. There was a festival to organize. At least that would take her mind off Craig. She walked toward the field again, where the next band was getting ready to play. Jon was about a hundred meters away. He lifted his arm and waved at Nina. But she was too sad to wave back.

Chapter 12

Breakdown on stage

The day was passing quickly. It was 9:30 p.m. and starting to get dark. Soon it would be time for Breakdown to play. Suddenly Nina realized something—she didn't care if she saw them play or not. She could walk out of here and go home. But she knew that was silly. Even though she was sad and hurt by Craig, she still wanted to make the day a success. If she didn't have Craig, at least she had her pride and self-respect! The crowds were coming. Some of them waved glowsticks in the air, lighting up the dark.

Nina walked toward the stage. Where was the music? Breakdown should be practicing by now, but there was no sound on the stage. Craig was hitting the drums, but the singer and the two guitarists were standing around. The amplifier and microphones weren't working. The singer shouted to Nina.

"Hey, lady! This sound system isn't working. Can you get someone to sort it out?"

She called Richard, who was on the other side of the field.

"Richard, there's a problem with the equipment. The power's not coming through to the amplifiers. Where's the sound man?"

"Oh no," Richard said. "I told him to go for a break about ten minutes ago. The sound was OK in rehearsal."

"Can you get him back? Text him or something. We need

him here right now."

Nina looked around her. The crowds were starting to get annoyed. Someone shouted. Someone else booed. If the sound man didn't come, the festival could be a disaster! People would ask for their money back. On the stage, Craig was standing up, preparing to leave.

"Wait a moment. I'm getting someone to fix the problem as fast as I can. Can't you help? Do you know anything about sound systems?"

"No," he said, "not me."

She looked behind him and saw Jon on the stage. What was he doing up there? He was looking down and moving different wires around. She ran over to him. "Can you fix it, Jon? Please tell me you can."

"I'm not sure . . . let me see . . . yes, that should do it. It's just some loose wires." He said to the singer, "Do a test on the microphone." The singer's voice came out strong and powerful. Yes, the microphone was working!

"Now try the guitar," Jon said. The guitarist played a chord and the sound could be heard loudly.

"They'll hear that in the next town! You're wonderful, Jon!" Nina cried.

All of the band members took their place on the stage. The crowd started cheering.

"Are you ready, Jambox?" the singer shouted. And the crowd cheered again. They began to play. Nina got lost in the music. They really were good—there was no doubt about that! She had been wrong about Craig. He wasn't interested in a relationship with her, but it was all right, she guessed.

"Are you OK?" It was Jon, standing behind her.

"Yes," Nina said. "I was just thinking that it's easy to be wrong about someone."

Jon laughed.

"Oh, I didn't mean *you*," Nina said, embarrassed.

"Does that mean you still think I'm a 'boring old businessman' only interested in money?"

"How did you . . . ?" Nina went red.

He laughed. "Your friend Marsha told me."

"But how . . . ?"

"She's my cousin."

"Your cousin! I'll kill her for not telling me."

"Blame me," Jon said. "I asked her not to say anything."

"I don't know what to say."

They sat down together on the grass. Nina spoke again. "Thanks for sorting out that problem with the loose wires. How did you know what to do?"

"I guessed one of the band members probably pulled them loose when they went up on stage. Perfectly logical really."

Nina laughed, liking Jon very much at that moment. "Are you always so logical about everything?"

"I can't help it. It's the way I am."

"Well, it's a good way to be," Nina said.

Perhaps I need to be a bit more logical and calm myself in the future, she thought.

MUSIC FESTIVAL
BREAK

She looked back at the stage. Craig was playing a drum solo. It was his special moment, and she could see the serious look on his face as his arms moved around with great skill and energy. The crowd shouted because they were enjoying it so much. One day he'd get that record contract he wanted so badly.

Soon Breakdown would be playing the last song.

"You're right, Nina. They are a very good band. You have a good ear." They watched the band in silence and then Jon moved slightly closer. "Come with me when this is finished and have something to eat. You must be really tired."

"OK, why not?"

"But first, let me show you this." Jon took out a piece of paper. "Look," he said, "I've just checked the ticket sales. With the profit you've made today, all your costs will be covered, no problem."

"Jon! Don't you ever stop thinking about business?"

"I'm not thinking about business anymore—not right now. How about you, Nina?"

Suddenly, her heart felt warm. "No, I'm not thinking about anything right now—apart from how hungry I am."

"So let's go for a nice meal and I promise not to talk business for the rest of the evening. Do we have a deal?"

"I'd like that," Nina said, smiling. "Yes, we have a deal!"

Review: Chapters 1–6

A. Match the characters in the story to the descriptions. You can use the names more than once.

Nina	Craig	Richard	Jon	Marsha

1. ____________ listens to a friend's problems.
2. went to Australia.
3. ____________ has a blog about music.
4. ____________ reports some bad news in a meeting.
5. ____________ and ____________ appear together in a photograph.
6. ____________ is the new owner of a large house.
7. ____________ rides a bike.
8. ____________ and ____________ are the festival organizers.

B. Circle the correct word or phrase in italics to complete each sentence.

1. Craig plays the (*guitar / drums / piano*).
2. Nina and Craig first met at (*college / a concert / work*).
3. The Jambox Festival is in (*April / August / May*).
4. Nina thinks the number of people at the festival will be (*the same as / higher than / lower than*) before.
5. (*Breakdown / Xray / Rolling Stones*) has played at the festival before.
6. Nina speaks to Jon Pritchard (*on the phone / in his office / in her office*).
7. Nina is (*surprised / excited / worried*) after her first meeting with Jon.
8. Jon wants (*some / all / half*) of the money before the festival.

C. Read the statements about the characters' feelings and decide if they are true (T) or false (F).

1. Marsha

a. is worried that Nina will be hurt by Craig. T / F

b. wants Nina and Craig to be together again. T / F

2. Richard

a. is confident that they can still use Huntley Manor for the festival. T / F

b. believes that they should cancel the festival. T / F

3. Nina

a. is attracted to Jon when they first meet. T / F

b. is shocked when she realizes that Jon wants to charge the festival organizers. T / F

D. Number these events in the order that they happened (1–7).

a. Nina has a meeting with Richard. _____

b. Nina leaves Jon's office feeling angry. _____

c. Nina goes backstage to see Craig. _____

d. Xray's manager calls Nina. _____

e. Nina changes the order of the bands. _____

f. Nina looks around Jon's land. _____

g. Nina cycles to Huntley Manor. _____

Review: Chapters 7–12

A. Number these events in the order that they happened (1–8).

a. Xray's manager is angry. ____
b. Nina argues with Marsha. ____
c. Nina hears Craig saying bad things about the festival. ____
d. Nina tries to find another venue. ____
e. There is a sound problem for Breakdown. ____
f. Jon makes a suggestion about ticket prices. ____
g. Jon invites Nina to go for dinner. ____
h. Nina sees Jon at the festival. ____

B. Look at each statement from the story and answer the questions.

1. "And I've cut the cost by 55 percent."
a. Who says this?
b. Who is this person speaking to?
c. Why do you think the speaker says this?

2. "I got you this. It's only a sandwich, I'm afraid . . ."
a. Who says this?
b. Who does the speaker give the sandwich to?
c. What does this show about the character's personality?

3. "I can't believe we agreed to play here!"
a. Who says this?
b. Who is this person speaking to?
c. Who else hears these words?

4. "I only said an agent *might* be here, . . ."
a. Who says this?
b. Who is this person speaking to?
c. What reaction does the speaker get?

5. "It's just some loose wires."
   a. Who says this?
   b. What problem is caused by the loose wires?
   c. Is the problem fixed?

6. "Your cousin! I'll kill her for not telling me."
   a. Who says this?
   b. What are the names of the cousins?
   c. Is the speaker serious or joking?

C. Circle the correct word or phrase in italics to complete each sentence.

1. When Nina meets Jon, she thinks he cares only about (*music / money / his land*).
2. Nina is (*angry / happy / sad*) when she reads Jon's email.
3. Nina goes (*swimming / running / cycling*) to forget about her problems.
4. Nina keeps daydreaming about (*Terry / Richard / Craig*).
5. Breakdown arrives (*early / on time / late*) for the festival.
6. Craig's DVD is for (*Nina / an agent / Jambox*).
7. Craig wants (*a relationship with Nina / to be successful in music / to form a new band*).

D. What do you think will happen after the end of the story? Think about these questions.

1. Will Nina and Jon start a relationship?
2. Will Craig be successful in music?

Answer Key

Chapters 1–6

A:
1. Marsha; **2.** Craig; **3.** Nina; **4.** Richard; **5.** Nina and Craig; **6.** Jon; **7.** Nina; **8.** Richard

B:
1. drums; **2.** college; **3.** August; **4.** higher than; **5.** Xray; **6.** in his office; **7.** excited; **8.** some

C:
1a. T; **1b.** F; **2a.** F; **2b.** F; **3a.** F; **3b.** T

D:
a. 4; **b.** 7; **c.** 1; **d.** 2; **e.** 3; **f.** 6; **g.** 5

Chapters 7–12

A:
a. 4; **b.** 2; **c.** 6; **d.** 1; **e.** 7; **f.** 3; **g.** 8; **h.** 5

B:
1. a. Jon; **b.** Nina; **c.** He feels sorry for Nina / He wants to help Nina.

2. a. Jon; **b.** Nina; **c.** He is kind/thoughtful/caring.

3. a. Craig; **b.** the other members of Breakdown; **c.** Nina

4. a. Nina; **b.** Craig; **c.** Craig is a bit angry and disappointed.

5. a. Jon; **b.** There is no sound; **c.** yes

6. a. Nina; **b.** Jon and Marsha; **c.** Nina is joking.

C:
1. money; **2.** angry; **3.** running; **4.** Craig; **5.** late; **6.** an agent; **7.** to be successful in music

D:
Answers will vary.

Background Reading:
Spotlight on . . . Music festivals

A. Read the information about the first music festival and answer the questions below.

Music at the Pythian Games

People often think that music festivals are a recent thing. Not exactly. Music festivals have been around for thousands of years.

The first music festival was held in Delphi, Greece, over 2,600 years ago. The Pythian Games, as they were later known, were held in honor of Apollo, the God of Music. In a competition lasting several days, musicians performed in the outdoor Theater of Delphi and the best performers were given the prize of a crown made of laurel leaves. This was a symbolic prize rather than a prize worth a lot of money.

Although music remained a central part of the games, other events were added later on, including art competitions, drama, and displays of physical strength, such as athletics. The Pythian Games were held every eight years and then every four years. The games were very popular and each time thousands of people came from the surrounding towns and cities to support their favorite performers. Delphi became known as an important city of music in Greece directly as a result of the Pythian Games.

1. Do you know any traditional events in the history of your country?
2. What do you enjoy watching best? Music, drama, or athletics?

B. Read the information about a modern festival in Britain and answer the questions below.

Greece to Glastonbury—the Past to the Present

Moving forward to modern times and to the birth of the world-famous Glastonbury musical festival in Somerset, England . . . The festival first took place in the summer of 1970 and was the idea of a farmer called Michael Eavis. Since the 1970s, the Glastonbury festival has taken place most years, and the audience has grown from 1,500 people to around 170,000. In the early days, the festival was free, but now the tickets have become very expensive. The festival lasts for three or four days, and many of the top musical acts like to play gigs at Glastonbury. But the Glastonbury festival is also a place where indie bands can take the stage and perform for their fans.

The British weather is so often rainy in the summer that many people associate Glastonbury with mud! The weather, however, doesn't stop people from coming. Visitors usually take a waterproof coat and a pair of rain boots, and prepare to enjoy themselves despite the rain.

Glastonbury, like other music festivals, is not usually a luxury holiday experience. People often sleep in a tent or a mobile home in the surrounding fields. The festival is not just for teenagers or young adults, but is popular with all age groups.

1. Should festivals like Glastonbury have cheap or even free tickets?
2. Would rainy weather stop you from going to Glastonbury or any other music festival?

Spotlight on . . . *Playing drums in a band*

A. Read the interview with Stacey Jones, a drummer from the band Party Rocksters, and answer the questions below.

Q: What's the best thing about being a professional drummer? And the worst?

A: Playing live is definitely the best thing! Nothing comes close to the feeling you get being on stage and hearing the reaction of the fans. I miss being away from home though. When you get back after a tour you realize you've missed important things, like a friend's birthday party, for example. You can feel a little bit on the outside and it takes a while to adjust to ordinary life again.

Q: How did you get started?

A: I had the chance to learn the drums at school and played in the school band. When I left school I was already playing gigs at weekends. So it started from there really.

Q: What advice would you give to other musicians?

A: This might sound obvious, but find the instrument that you really enjoy playing. It's no good practicing the saxophone if you really want to be a drummer. Because I'm a girl, people were a bit surprised when I said I wanted to be a drummer, but I'm glad I didn't let anyone put me off.

1. If you could interview any musician, who would you choose? What questions would you ask?
2. Would you like to play a musical instrument professionally? Why? Why not?

B. Now read about Stacey's schedule and answer the questions below.

A Typical Day on Tour

When I'm on tour with the band, it's all a bit crazy. Normally I get up at seven in the morning and go for a run, but when I'm on the road and staying in a hotel, we have breakfast brought to our rooms—at about 10 a.m. At home I have a piece of toast, but I need a lot more food on tour, so I'll have some eggs and maybe some fish to keep me going. I find my body burns up a lot of energy when I'm actually playing on stage, and if I don't have a good diet with proteins and carbohydrates, then I won't be able to do the full set of songs.

After breakfast, I go to the hotel gym and lift some weights. As a drummer, I use my arms a lot in this job, so I mainly do stuff for my upper body, as well as press-ups. It's important to stay fit. I also go on the running and cycling machines to build up my stamina.

The hardest part of the day is early afternoon. When I've had lunch and there's not much to do it can get boring. I might watch a film in my hotel room or play Scrabble with some of the band members. Sometimes I'll have a little sleep.

By about 5 p.m. I start to get excited about that night's performance—and also a little nervous! I hate eating before I go on stage so I'll have a pizza or something afterwards with the band. Then we get to bed at about 2 a.m. before it all starts again.

1. Does Stacey's life on the road sound appealing to you or not?
2. Do you think Stacey has a healthy lifestyle?

Glossary

agent (*n.*) a person or business authorized to act on behalf of another. A band, a performer, or an author usually has an agent.

atmosphere (*n.*) a feeling or mood in a room or area

(top) billing (*n.*) the position in which a performer or act is listed on posters. The performer who gets top billing goes on stage last.

blogger (*n.*) a person who writes a blog, a website containing the writer's or group of writers' own experiences, observations, opinions, etc.

budget (*n.*) the total sum of money set aside or needed for a purpose

cancel (*v.*) to decide that a planned event will not take place

cheer (*v.*) to shout encouragement

committee (*n.*) a group of people elected or appointed to perform a specified service or function

disappointed (*adj.*) sad because something was not as good as expected

electrician (*n.*) a person whose job is the installation, maintenance, and repair of electrical devices

gig (*n.*) a musical performance

indie band (*n.*) a group (of musicians) who do not have a contract with a record company

lineup (*n.*) a list of performers

logical (*adj.*) reasonable or sensible

muddy (*adj.*) covered with wet dirt

profit	(*n.*)	surplus money in a business after all charges are paid
reception	(*n.*)	an area in an office, hotel, etc., where visitors or guests are received, and appointments or reservations are dealt with
record contract	(*n.*)	an agreement to make musical recordings, i.e., songs
stage	(*n.*)	the platform on which the actors or musicians perform
support act	(*n.*)	the performer who goes on stage before the main act
venue	(*n.*)	the place where a concert, musical performance, or other event happens

NOTES